Moments & Lifetimes

A collection of the ones
I turned into poetry

Meagan Murtaugh

Cover Art by Ellie Meisner

DEDICATION

To the ones who helped heal my broken heart.

CONTENTS

1   Prelude   9

2   The Ones Who Were Moments   Pg 13

3   The Ones Who Were a Lifetime   Pg 79

PRELUDE

If you fall in love with me,
I'll turn you into poetry.

You'll be forever stuck
between the lines on this paper.

WERE WE A MOMENT OR A LIFETIME?

THE ONES WHO WERE MOMENTS…

Somewhere between our first "hello,"
and our final "goodbye,"

I found a piece of me that was missing.

You said it was always going to be
you and me.

Your words.
They made me black out the parts
I was meant to see.
Now I'm frozen.

I'm trapped inside our memories.

Maybe in another dimension,
I would have finally got your attention.
Maybe in the multiverse,
you and me would have actually worked.

He wore his scars like armor.

And that's when I realized,
we never had a chance.

I used to fill books with your name.
Each line eventually started to look the same.
My words about you
went from colorful to beige.
Now you're nothing more to me than a

(blank page).

Learning to breathe again.
Because you were my lungs.

Stitched myself up
without your pity or help.

You broke me in all the right places.

I stay awake through the pain
and all the heavy rain,
just to feel that missing piece of you.

I smell your scent
on my pillows and sheets.

And I can't comprehend
that the last time I saw you
was the last time we would meet.

All this time
you had me straddling a very thin line.
I finally removed the filter between us
and accepted that

you were never really mine.

I wanted him to be it.
But instead,
he was the one who showed me
where all the pieces are supposed to fit.

Maybe you weren't "the one."

But at least you were the one
who took me out of these broken shadows,
and showed me the rising sun.

Like a distant memory,
you'll always hold a piece of me.
Our souls collided and instantly caught flames,
but our fire was put out by the pouring rain.

I'm holding onto a wet match,
just hoping it'll spark again.
My head up to the sky,
begging the universe to explain.

(We could have held the world in our hands).

Everything you said
turned into an alibi.
We'll never understand
why it's so hard to say goodbye.

I almost gave you everything and more.
But then I realized,
I'd never win that inner war.

Not sure why I fall in love with people
with this trait.
They're present in the moment,
but it feels like we'll never match each other's fate.

I beg the universe for a common soul.
Someone whose heart beats just as full.

I stand alone in a crowded room.
When the only one I want to show up...

is you.

Everything about me and you
is blurry.
The stars burn at the thought of us.
They drop from the sky in a cloudy haze
while I get sick of counting the days
until you finally decide
to hold on to me

or let me go.

I made his world too loud.
He wasn't ready for the perfect storm.

My minds been aching.
Because everything is changing.
Thought I was done with these tests.
Found a home in his eyes
where I could finally rest.

It felt like a lifetime.
But it was gone in an instant.
What was once clear to me
is now fading in the distance.

Feels like I'm living in someone else's dreams.
I close my eyes
and there you are.

I close my eyes
just to keep us alive.

Our memories are fossilized,
Leaving imprints on my heart
that will eventually crystalize.

And turn to dust.

In my dreams,
but out of reach.
Lying here wishing you knew.
But also wishing
there was something I could take
to help me forget you.

Built it up
just to watch it fall.
A part of me thought you were worth
risking it all.
Broke my silence
when I stopped fighting back.

Every image of you has faded to black.

You were always the earth.
And I was the rain.

And I got sick of helping you survive.

Fading in and out of reality.
Lost in time
and hoping it stops when you reach me.
Even when I lose all sense of sound,
I still feel you.
I still feel you all around.

I've finally accepted that
my soul was always too deep
for those who only want
to swim in the shallow end.

So many words.
So many words I've written,
but never said.
So much black smoke
fills the empty spaces in my head.
Spaces I left for you.

Until I pronounced us dead.

All we are is skin and bones
just trying to find a warm body
to make us whole.

I hope you think of me.
Especially in those moments when
you see an *almost* perfect sunset
and it reminds you of how we were
almost perfect.

There's an ocean between us
and you keep telling me to swim.

Why am I always the only one
gasping for air?

You were an unfinished story
in my playbook.
A rough draft crumpled in the corner
that would never get a second look.

You treat us like we have so much time.
Until one day,

we flatline.

I gave you the world,
but you let it go.
Now every time we talk about me,
you black out like you don't wanna know.

Please stop wishing me well.
Stop saying you're happy for me.

You knew I'd move on
the moment you set my heart free.

Everything is changing.
Those moments from the past;
they're fading.

And once again you sit beside me
in silence

just letting them fade.

I can't help but feel your soul
especially when I miss it most.
Every day.
It's like I'm still here with your ghost.

Felt the earth shift when I finally walked away.
Traded in my scars
for sunsets and better days.

Wondering if there is something I can do.
Something new we can try.
Because I just want to escape
with you for one more night.

I wish on every universe that
ours will collide one day.
But until that day comes,
it just feels like you are worlds away.

My lungs are tired
from breathing you in.
My bones ache
from holding on.

Our names were written in stone,
until you threw it against the wall
and it broke into millions of pieces.

I fell apart
trying to keep it all together
for you.

They wrote me a letter once,
but the words have now faded.

The only part that I remember
was when they signed it
"Always and forever."

(Another lie trapped in ink).

He made her mascara run.
So, she left him with nothing
but red lipstick stains on his pillow.

A reminder to lay in the bed he made.

You left me in flames
just waiting for a reply.

You will always be the most beautiful lie.

I thought the roots we planted
would never rip once they grew.
I thought it would always be
me and you.

You left me free falling
and I'm not sure where this ends.
I would crawl back to you,
but I'm too far down
and can't seem to break through.
These lucid dreams are too vivid to comprehend.

Wake me up.
Dig me out.
This can't be it.
(This can't be the end).

The sky turned grey and cried tears of joy.
It washed away every memory of you.

The last light on the horizon faded.
And I sat there smiling,
as the world turned black
on everything we had created.

(*a sign from the universe it was finally time to move on*).

The rain poured down that morning
and I remember every last drop
that touched my skin.

Tried to hold my breath,
but felt the walls caving in.

Let the water fill my lungs
thinking maybe it would cleanse me of you.

My lips touched the surface
as the world took hold of me.
I looked around and saw nothing…

That's when I knew I was finally free.

Watched the clouds fade to black
while your face drifted towards the back.

Felt destiny bring out the best of me...

While you just stayed the same.

Broken memories resurface when I think
of what could have been.

You could have taken my half-filled heart,
and made it whole again.

You keep trying to take away
the parts you want from me.
But still, I sit here alone in this city.
Surrounded by noise and static.

Tell me.
Why does everything about you have to be so

overly
dramatic?

I think I'm finally done.
Done holding you inside my mind
hoping you show up one night.
You won't and it's fine.

The sky might be falling,
But the stars in my eyes still shine.

You only want me when I'm hard to see.
Only reaching out when I'm the best version of me.
It's like you're afraid to lose me,
but not enough to keep me around.
And every time I lose you,
you make it so easy to be found.

You only.
You only love me when you're lonely.

My pulse was ever changing.
You gave me the highest highs,
but you trapped me in the lowest lows.

I finally escaped the mistakes you made.
You'll never change.

Let's just call a spade a spade.

Even though it felt so sudden,
I guess I should have seen it coming.
Like a shock wave in the dark of night,
you disappeared faster than the speed of sound.

Your ray of light…

Nowhere to be found.

You never should have let me go.

Now I'm someone that you'll never know.

Watched the light fade away
in the distance.
(I always knew you'd never stay).
Saw nothing but your eyes in the black out.

Now you're someone I guess I'll learn to live without.

Maybe we'll meet again in another life.
I'll run to you with open arms.
We won't even have to question it this time.
Everything will just make sense.
The stars will instantly align.

I'll be yours.
And you'll be mine.

Another restless night
just lying next to the ghost of you.
I want to close my eyes.
I want to sleep on my own.

I want to go one day without fearing the unknown.

This would never work.

I see the world through a kaleidoscope lens,
and you are colorblind.

It's sinking in
that this could really be over.
You keep showing up every time I'm barely sober.
You know deep down
I hate that you're gone.
No matter what we do…

You'll keep getting lost in me.
And I'll keep letting you.

Make it count.
I want to remember the way you hurt me.
Claw my heart out one last time.

(A blessing in disguise).

Your bittersweet crime.

You wrote words in the sand
and then you watched me
watch them as they washed away.

You told me to look for buried treasures another day.

If I crossed oceans to get to you,
would it even matter?

Because I really don't know if you're worth sinking for.

We never know how to say goodbye.
So instead, we pour different colors of permanent ink
into our separate worlds,
and mix it together like tie dye.
I wear you to sleep.
I smell you on my skin.
The sweatshirt you left here
is nice and worn in.
I wash it to erase you,
but I'll never know how.
I'll just keep breathing you in
until my body begins to ache.
I'll just keep breathing you in
until the memories of you disintegrate.

You cursed the moon
when you walked away.
Leaving traces of ink
where your soul was meant to stay.

And in that moment
where you left it all behind,
I was ready to cradle your heart,
but all you did was break mine.

When I'm around you
my heart beats faster.
And I can't decide if it's love,
or just another disaster.

People tell me I deserve the world.
But what if the one I want is the universe?

THE ONES WHO WERE A LIFETIME…

I count the days.
They pass so slow.
Never knew where you were before.
But if I've waited this many lifetimes
to find you,
I'd wait thousands more.

Dreams used to be better
when I was asleep.
With him, I was lonely.
But with you my world moves slowly.
I talk to the stars.
I tell them all about you.
I carve your name in the sky
with the light from within.

I forget where I used to be.
I forget where I've been.

Felt kind of lonely before you,
but now it's like I've never been.

Was drowning in darkness,
until you pulled my light from within.

It wasn't just that he held my heart
like it was made of glass.
It was all the things
he did
to keep it from breaking.

You've got the world in your hands,
but you're scared I'll walk away.

I've got my hands on your heart,
and I'm telling you I'll stay.

He made perfect sense
and then no sense at all
at the exact same time.

He was beautiful chaos.

Our souls are so far past the clouds that we end up in space.
But I hold onto to the light separating our fingers
just in case.

Take me away.

I'll follow you to another universe.
Somewhere in the multiverse.
Somewhere far beyond this world's creation
lies a universe of cosmic imagination.

We can breathe in the stardust that orbits the curves in our lips.
Watch the planets surrounding our bodies
speak to us in waves while our hearts do back flips.

I see us.
Sitting on the moon.
My head resting on your shoulder while we watch the people below.
Nothing else matters.
I just want these memories with you to overflow.

Your mind and my mind.
Your soul and my soul.

This could be our new reality.

Defying all types of gravity.

If I could bottle up
that feeling I get
when you walk into a room
and bring it with me everywhere,

I know I'd hold the universe
in the palms of my hands.

Sometimes I wonder,
who would I be
if I had never held your hand?

I'm sinking below the surface
with every word
that you whisper.

I'm losing myself in you.

Cleaning up the mess inside my head
before you're someone I leave behind.
In so deep
and I might be scared to fall,
but for you

I'd risk it all.

I watched the world happen
all around me,
and the only thing that made sense
was the way my soul lit up
when I thought of yours.

I want to touch the sky
with you tonight.
Your eyes keep finding mine like a satellite.

I'm done being afraid.
I'm done trying to hide.
Let's meet where the stars in our souls collide.

You were the twist in my story.
The chapter I didn't know the words to.
And once I started to read,
there was no going back.

I like that you fill all the cold spaces
in between my fingers.
I like having something
to hold onto.

The last thing on my mind
before I close my eyes at night.
In my head
and in my dreams.
You're the last image I see
before I drift off to sleep.

Starting to think we might have it.
I'm writing things down
to remember this thought.
I'm keeping certain pages hidden
so I don't get caught.

I'm turning the stars into galaxies
in the forefront of my imagination.

The reality of it all,
is that I'm waiting for the universe
to make us
it's next miraculous creation.

If I could do anything,
I'd find a way to freeze these moments with you.
I'd let your eyes melt into mine.
I'd turn back time.

We could be oceans away
and still see the same sunrise.

We could go blind the next day,
and still remember
the look in each other's eyes.

I think there's nirvana in his energy.
Or maybe in his eyes.
But the shockwave to my multiverse
took my soul by surprise.

I wandered for you
while the stars breathed me in.
Broke the barrier between
reality and my vast imagination.

When I look for the light
that's meant to guide me home,

I'll look for you.

You're my constellation.

There's something beautiful
about the way
we were once scattered into
millions of pieces.

Maybe it's because you found me
when I was putting myself
back together again.
Or maybe it's because our souls
spoke languages to each other
that at the time
we couldn't comprehend.

But you took this fragile heart
and wrapped in sheets of gold.
You erased the broken pieces of my past
and ignited the light back into my soul.

I know it sounds crazy,
but I am certain that we met in another life.
Because when I look into your eyes
it's a familiar feeling that only
the two of us could ever recognize.

I used to think that home was a place,
until I realized that home is actually us.

Home is this exact moment that was created
by other little moments
between you and me.

The moments that will forever be mental pictures
inscribed in my heart and in my soul.
The moments where I look at your face,
and I remember that this is the reason
I am finally whole.

There's something beautiful
about the promises we are making today.
And if I had to promise you one thing, it's this:

Wherever you go, I'll go.
Wherever you stay, I'll stay.

You held my heart in your hands.
I went from standing still
to our very first dance.

I'm jealous of the stars
because they knew about us
before we ever did.

Sometimes when it rains,
I ask myself if this part of the earth
is brand new,
or if it's already touched your lips
in another lifetime.

Stopped looking when you came along.
Was used to thinking of things I could do alone.
You appeared in the dark
through the pouring rain.
The glimmer of light
that outshined by pain.

My soul is half asleep
and dreaming of you.

Felt alive when I opened my eyes.
You became someone
I couldn't breathe without.
Inhaled every piece of your soul.
Exhaled all of my old doubt.

I feel you in my bones.
I breathe you in when I close my eyes.
The blood that swirls through my veins.
The smell in the air after it rains.

You are everything that brings me to life.

The person I am now
is someone I've never been.

Wouldn't it be beautiful to let the right one in?

I feel you in another dimension
every time I close my eyes.
I wish you could make it here somehow
because I'd show you the galaxies we would live in now.
I'd shatter the surface that separates
our realities and our dreams.

For you.
I'd rip open the universe at the seams.

Your eyes tell me all of the
beautiful stories
I've heard of,
but never had the chance to read.

Until you walked into my life so unexpectedly.

On those days
that darkness tries to find me,
I look for you.

The light that leads me home.

Even with certain pieces
scattered all over the floor,
we still manage to fit perfectly
in this chaotically beautiful mess
we made together.

We watched the sky shed
millions of layers that night.

And I want to be like the sky
when I'm with you.

I wake in the night
and think of your face.
The whole world is sleeping,
but my whole world is you.

You said your mind is a prison,
and I want to break through.

My mind is the ocean,
and I'm drowning in you.

Lost in this moment
set inside your eyes.

But still, I can't wait for
every tomorrow with you.

The world we used to know
is now an entirely different view.

We are showing all of our beautiful flaws.
Slowly tearing down every wall.
Just stay with me for the whole ride.
We can be weightless under
each other's sky.

I was broken, wild and free.
So blind I couldn't see.

Until I felt your air soft on my skin.
(You make me high).
I just want to keep breathing you in.

It's like you already heard
the beating of my heart.

You already felt the lining in my soul.

I will take the parts of yourself
that you don't love
and I will love them enough
for the both of us.

Someone asked me today,
"How do you know when someone is good for you?"

It's simple.

They make you breathe the world in differently.

Feeling stuck inside my mind.
So here I am…
I'm leaving all my wounds open again.

Afraid to bleed out.
I can't pretend.
But there's something about you
that makes me know I won't break.

So, for you,

I'll bend.

Was afraid this all would fade,
but instead, it's falling into place.
So now I'm sitting here
with my lungs tight in my chest
trying to find new ways to breathe.
Trying to believe.

He looked over at me
as if I had just hand painted the sky.

And I thought,
how wonderful is it,
to be thought of as someone
who brings sunsets to another person's eyes
just by showing up.

Memorized the touch of your skin.
Savoring every moment.
I keep breathing you in.
I watch the sun set each night
because I can't wait for tomorrow.

Wherever you go,
my heart will follow.

Losing myself in your eyes tonight.
Drifting towards the brightest of lights.
Thinking about you and me.
You lift my soul to another galaxy.

I fell for the way
you spoke to my soul
in a language it's never heard before.

It blacked out the pieces of my past
I try so hard not to think of anymore.

And on some days,
I feel you in my bones.

With every move I make.

You are a part of me.

*I was once scattered into millions
of pieces,
and now I am whole again.*

*I found beauty
in all the times I fell apart.*